Get a Life

by Hermann Traub

Published in Great Britain by
KEVIN MAYHEW LIMITED
Rattlesden, Bury St Edmunds
Suffolk IP30 0SZ
ISBN 0 86209 799 1
Cat. No. 1500048

Printed in Germany 1996

Foreword

'Get a life!' we say, when we are telling someone to wake up and start living.

That is exactly what this book is about –
but it's about a life which is far more exciting,
challenging and fulfilling than anything everyday
existence has to offer.

It's a life with Jesus Christ –
a life of commitment to the highest;
a life to be lived to the full.

Get a life!

Free at Last

Free at last,
pushing off from the shore,
great waters before you,
a boat for your journey,
unlimited supplies,
and paddles that will not
break.

Free at last,
pushing off from the shore
of boredom,
great waters of opportunity
before you,
in the spacious boat of life,
carrying all that you need
and powered by an
unbreakable spirit.

Free at last,
but with a compass
that will allow you
to find your way home.

Free at last,
but with a friend
who will share your
journey.

Free at last,
but not without a lifeline
to be thrown to you
should you ever go under.

If you never trust yourself
to the wind,
you will stay where you are,
becalmed and going
nowhere.

If you cannot see the light of
heaven,
you will never find your way
along the paths of earth.

If you do not know what it
means to be free,
you are not equipped for
responsibility.

So this is my wish for you –
that you learn to trust in
God.
He will provide you with the
wind of his Spirit.
He will give you light for the
next step.
He will give you freedom for all
life's tasks.

Give Your Love Time

I stood with my camera ready. The sky promised a sunset on the sea that I didn't want to miss. The clouds were bathed darkly in lilac and blue. I focussed my camera on the solar disc, and waited for it to dip towards the sea, catching picture after picture on my film. I could hardly wait for that glorious moment when sun and sea would meet in glowing gold. But every second seemed an age; the sun was moving too slowly; my film was quickly running out; and now, the big moment had arrived for the best picture of all. I pressed the button. No response. The film was finished. And so I missed the picture I'd been hoping for.

In the case of the sunset, it is not tragic, but in life, it is. You want an example? Boy meets girl. They are attracted to each other. They come to love and trust each other, to understand each other.

Holding hands is at first real happiness. But the boy begins to be impatient. He wants not only a kiss, but everything. She still needs time for love. Should he allow her this time? Should he hold back and wait? Or should he insist on finishing the film of his love too quickly and too soon? Then their love will run out, before it has the chance to mature.

You have time. Allow the one you love to have time too. There is a right time for everything. Love needs time. We all need love. But many have destroyed their love before its time had come.

I am not going to saw through
the branch on which I am sitting;
and though they laugh at me when I tell
them that I talked to God today,
I will not stop praying.

I am not going to allow
my life's potential to be blighted;
and though they laugh because I won't swallow
the pill that makes them feel good,
I will stand firm, and say no.

I am not going to let my eye
become blinded to beauty and colour;
and if they laugh at me because
I haven't slept around,
I will still wait for the one I truly love,
and who loves me.

My God,
when I am really in full swing
and travelling is a thrill,
then I cry out for sheer joy
with the love of life.

My God,
when I'm really filled with joy
and know that life's worth living,
then I gladly praise your name
for the happiness I feel.

My God,
when I come back down to earth
and my legs are weak and trembling,
then you keep me firm and steady
with a hold that is sure.

SANT UZ BEACH
BOAR WALK

When Everything is in Bloom

Youth is full of blossoming colour;
let nobody spoil your beauty.

Youth is full of strength and courage;
let no one destroy your dreams.

Youth is full of ups and downs;
let no one upset your buoyancy.

Youth is full of hope and trust;
let no one dissuade you from faith.

Equipped for Life

When I have the right footwear
I can walk along paths
seldom trodden.

When I have a firm faith,
I can make bold decisions
seldom taken.

When I have a lasting love,
I can cross desert wastes
seldom travelled.

With Jesus
at your side
you'll have firm faith
and lasting love.

Go with him
along the way;
he is waiting
at your door.

A beautiful country road through an avenue of trees is just the place for a pleasant afternoon walk or ride out in the car. Nothing could be more peaceful or enjoyable. But how easily it can all be spoilt by selfish carelessness. A speeding driver, with no interest in the attractions of the scene, tears down the road as if it were a race track, doesn't see the family walking near the verge, skids and crashes into a tree, his car bursting into flames. In a moment, paradise has turned into hell; a place of pleasure becomes a place of pain. How easily are the good things in life turned into the bad. It happens all the time.

A stimulating glass of wine is one of life's pleasures, but to the alcoholic it is fatal, and we all know the damage done by alcohol abuse.

It is good to have ambitions in life, but when ambition becomes ruthless obsession it crushes all in its path.

Friendship is wonderful, but if your friends lead you astray you are better off without them.

Worship is the highest human goal, but if you worship the wrong gods they end up by destroying you.

I will measure my
strength.
I will test my
stamina.
I will push myself
to the limit.
I will discover just
what I can do.

Jesus is not against you
proving your strength.

Pushing across boundaries
is part of his programme.

You can test yourself to the limit
by accepting his promises.

Living with him
is full of adventure.

Don't think too small
about yourself
and Jesus.

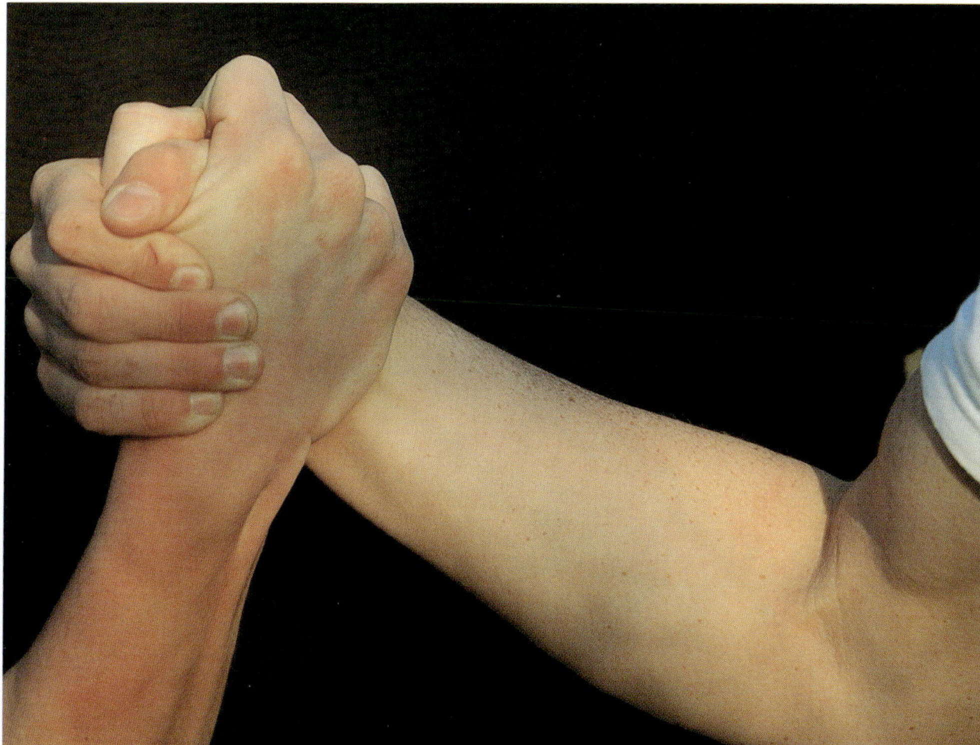

A Sense of Direction

Sooner or later you have to decide what you're aiming for.
You must set the points on the track of your life
to decide the direction in which you want to travel.
Set your points towards what is good.
Steer away from what is bad.

There's your career to consider.
What can you do? What do you want to do?
How will you earn your living?

There are relationships too;
above all, who is the one you are looking for
to share the rest of your life?

Yes, the track of your life is stretching out before you.
But it is not a fixed route that you *have* to travel.
There are many crucial points when you must stop
and choose the right direction.
Sometimes it will be easy, sometimes hard.
Ask God to help. He knows the way.

15

You stand out
because you are
unique.
You stand out
because you wear
a different colour.
You are marvellously
distinct from
everything
around you.

To God you are special;
to him you are unique;
the remarkable original
he intended you to be.

So don't be a conformist,
the same as everyone else;
don't adapt to your surroundings,
be yourself.

'Thank you, Lord,
for making me so different
and unique.'

A Letter

Dear....

You look so very tired – or is it my imagination? Perhaps you have come a long way. But here are a few stones to rest on. You don't have much luggage, I see. Perhaps a bar of chocolate. You must be thirsty, but you haven't found a well with clean water. And you are looking for a well – not only for now, but for your whole life. When love dries up, you'll want a well of love. When courage fails, a well of courage; fresh springs of hope, when hope is all but dead.

I know of such a well that never dries. I drink from it every day. And it isn't far away. It is the Word of God. In it are springs of living water to refresh your spirit's weariness. In it you meet the Friend who will travel with you on the road.

The Wallflower

Is there any point
in flowering so inconspicuously
in the shadow of a wall
almost unobserved?

Is there any point
in living so timidly
in the shadow of the great,
unnoticed and unknown?

Is there any point
in just being hidden
behind the shadow of success,
unrecognised and ignored?

Surely God has called you
to bring you out of the shadows
of a life that means nothing.

Surely God has called you
to move you out of the shadows
of sleepy inertia.

Surely God has called you
from the dark and empty shadows
because he knows the potential
waiting within you
to be born.

I want to reach the next milestone.
Why else am I riding this bike?
Why else am I using my energy?
For what other reason am I
breathing so hard?

I want to reach the next milestone.
Why else have I heard God's word?
Why else do I spend my time
with Christians?
Why else have I received new love?

I want to reach the next milestone.
Why else have I made my
commitment?
Why else have I found new horizons?
For what other reason have I found
a way to God?

FUNK

Picture Credits

Cover Picture: R. Haak

p.5 left: P. Jacobs; p.5 right: R. Haak; p.7 left: L. Hartmann; p.7 right: Bertrand Photographic Archives; p.8: W. Okon; p.9: W. Rauch; p.11 left: L. Lenz; p.11 right: C. Palma; p.12: W. Rauch; p.13 R. Haak; p.15 left: N. Kustos; p.15 right: Deuter/IFA picture team; p.16: H. Herfort; p.17: U. Kröner; p.19 left: C. Baumgartner; p.19 right: W. Rauch; p.20: K. Radtke; p.21: P. Santor; p.23: W. Köhler; pp.24, 25: M. Zweigle; p. 27 left: P. Santor; p.27 right: K. Radtke; p.28: M. Leppert; p.29: M. Will; p.30: P. Santor; p.31: Endler/IFA picture team